UNSETETOBOLE

THE ONE BLOCK

THE FIRST EPIC NOVEL

Arya

Clever Fox
PUBLISHING
Chennai • Bangalore

CLEVER FOX PUBLISHING
Chennai, India

Published by CLEVER FOX PUBLISHING 2021

ISBN: 978-93-93229-05-2

THE iNTRO

Spot the names in Novel

Normal character

Astro:

The Cyborg's Partner. Alerts the Hero of Evil.

Main Character

Cyborg: A Helpful Hero! Fights back when an unexpected problem comes.

Villains of Problem

Alen 1: Villain who is not smart, but he the villan.

Alen 2, 3, 4, 5, 6, 7,8,9,10: Alen 1's crew but annoys him sometimes.

Tyee: Fiction Season 1
Unsetewbole.
THe one block
begining

Chapter 1

THE BEGINNING OF THE WAR

It was a very peaceful day for planet Earth.

No, not quiet day. I mean "No Problems", people playing, no distraction. But now it is about the alens.

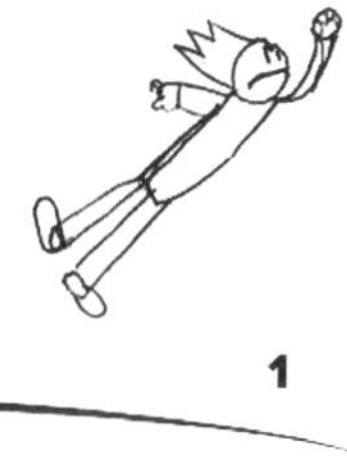

Meanwhile, at a nearby planet things were getting worse for the alens. They hate planet Earth.

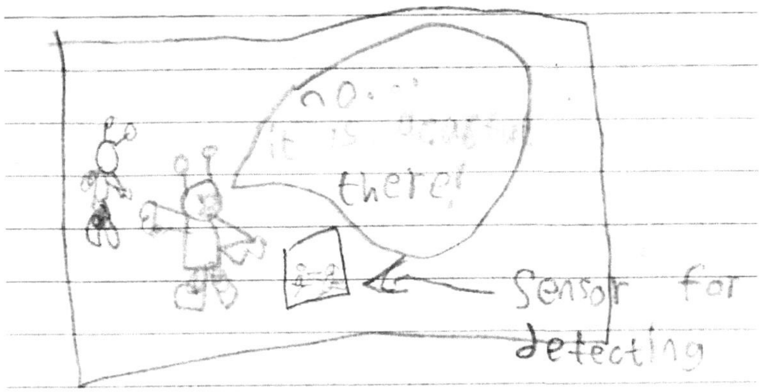

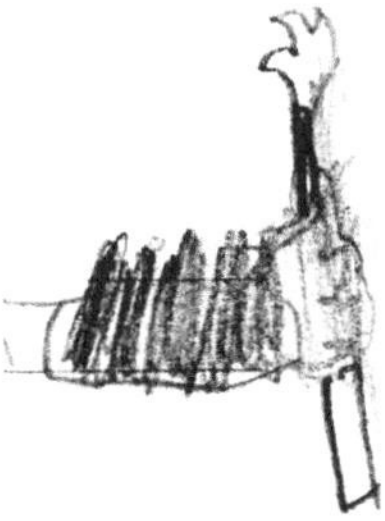

They thought of inventing a weapon:

Like doublizer, triplizer, quatruplizer horror.

A weapon that can make only One Block just like platforming.

So they began on a mission to find a metal and began digging in the mines. They also need iron and a furnace to smelt the iron and colour to dye the weapon. They made a list of what they need, but stay tuned! Because new things will be added in the list. I can provide just this that the weapon will be called

"THE ONE BLOCK CONVERTER"

Back to planet Earth. Meanwhile, at a giant Space Shuttle, an Astronaut was thinking. Before I take flight, I would like to quickly take a look at the outer space with a Telescope. So he got his telescope and began looking, and the Space Shuttle was now set to take flight in 1:30:3:13:24 by that Astronomer and he saw a strange planet.

He'd like to make an article about the thing he just saw, and so it appeared in the newspaper and they have been crazy! Meanwhile, at the alens' planet, they have given their best to find two stones. Yes, because the stone is rare in the alens' planet. After searching for hours together they finally found a rare stone, they only need one stone and make it back home to the mines. But back to the mines, Why? Because they need iron, other ores and one more rare stone. It took hours and hours to find the second stone but then a paper fell down from the skies...

They grabbed it, "Huh? What's this?", shouted alen 1 in horror. The paper said that:

"To alen 1

A new strange ore came out today. It is said that it can upgrade any weapon or create any weapon. Mash the ore and turn it into a drink. If you drink it, the mind will search for the weapon that you are trying to make. Just say any number from 1 to 20, and also luckily, it lives on our planet. But remember to keep this as a secret.

-From Alen 21202."

"This is a fortune!", said alen 1. "Lets search for the ore! But let's finish the work and soon the humans will have a hard time! Let's go".

The New Ore looked like this:

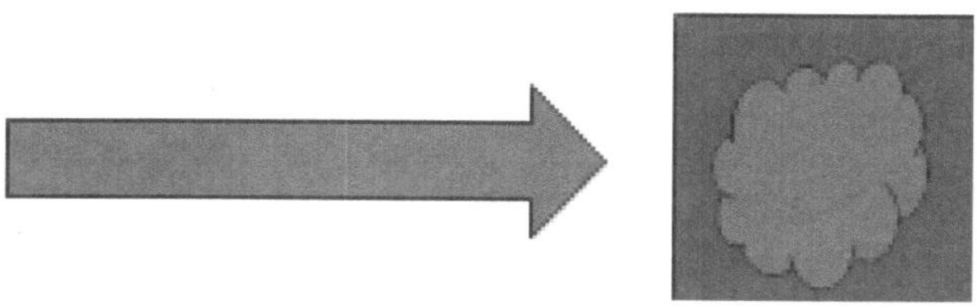

But they have to dig deeper. But now they have worked hard enough and made it back to their home.

Their result:

4 X 3 stones,

1 iron and

0 new ore.

Then back to earth, in Sai Street, capital of steel island, a cyborg from the future had seen something strange, that in a nearby planet some unknown creatures. Guess what you're about to discover? It was alens planet! The cyborg went to the Astronomer and the cyborg said, "I found strange creatures in the planet from the article you wrote!" "Really!," asked the Astronaut. Then show me a proof. "OK"! said the cyborg he used his eyes to project a large screen.

And so he understood that the cyborg was telling the truth and it played out in the news. They (people) were shocked: no, not an electric shock! the surprised shock.

The alens had so much rest so, they continued. Then they got distracted by seeing.... diamonds! Then alen 1, the leader of the alens, had an idea. "Thankfully, we had this checklist. Let's add those diamonds to our check list !" gasped alen 1. They mined the diamonds and ticked diamonds. They had another idea. They were thinking of pearl, like season ten of pokemon: "Diamond and Pearl", like when.... oh never mind lets continue. They turned the paper.

THE NEXT 50

In the back of the paper:

The secret in the back of this paper to alen 1.

About pearl:

Pearl... Pearl is located in a blue mine. You will find it somewhere in the mine. The pearl is purple, a strange colour. But since it is a big mine it will be difficult for you to find, but there is a goggle that can help you find it, so bye.

-From Alen 100."

Pearl is perfect! Time to add it in our list. And so alen 1 wrote "Pearl" in their check list and then they began looking for a blue cave, and also, lol, it is not paper. It is their tab. You just got pranked! P.S.: if you don't like it then ignore it or find something to cheer you up. But when I said the paper fell down, it was not a joke. It was real. It is not April fools anyway.

Real look of the TAB:

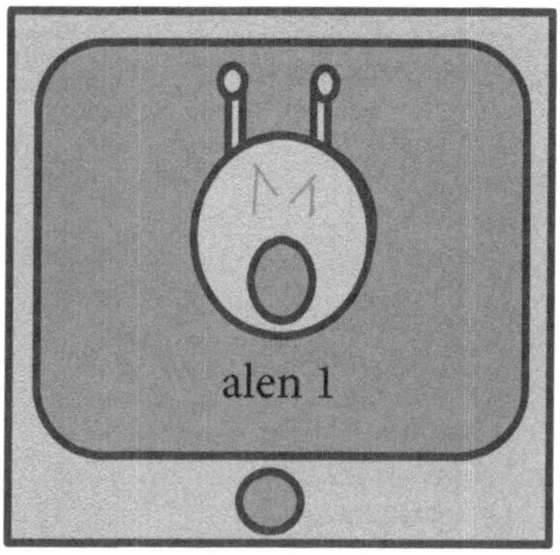

P.S.: unless you are reading it in April fools day.

Now the space shuttle will take 1 hour before flight along with the cyborg because he is so useful! Yep!, guess what? Sadly the alens had found the blue cave! But it has not been long until the alens got busted! The cyborg luckily spotted them red-handed. Ring, ring! The cyborg alarmed the Astros in short. "Wake up!", shouted the cyborg to the Astros. "What is it?", asked the Astros. "The creatures are now finding the magical pearl!", said the cyborg. "I want to see it!", replied the Astros. The cyborg handed a disk and placed it in the telescope and it showed the alens finding pearl and zoomed into the checklist.

And here are their results (currently), No, no, no!

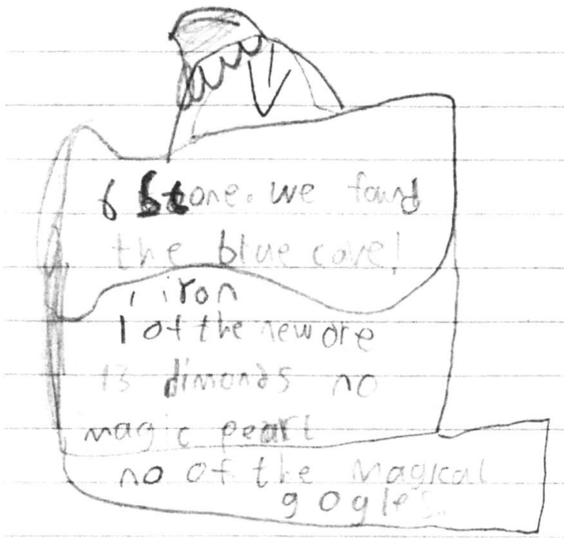

P.S.: We will show how the pearl looked like when they found pearl. I hope you understand, but no skipping pages! That is cheating.

But they found the magical ore! It is not just alen 1 who found the ore, it was other 13 alens.

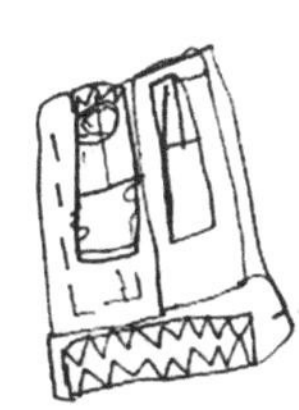

Anyway, lets dust off the alens and go to the cyborg and Astros. When people around the world were getting information from the Astros and cyborg about the alens and what they are doing with the checklist. People started screaming and running like lunatics.

Then the alens found the mysterious pearl mission complete! "Now let's build the weapon!", said alen 1. "But what about the goggles?", said alen 3. "Hmmm.... we might need them!", said alen 1. So, he picked up the goggles and went back up to the surface. "Where should we build the weapon?", asked alen 2. "Simple! Just follow me!", said alen 1. "Racum! Racum! Open up", Shouted alen 1. Suddenly a staircase opened. "What's down there?", shouted alen 5. "Relax! Don't be a scary cat! I'll activate the lights with another magic word! and.... everything will be fine, ok!?", said alen 1. Here we go..... kill darkness exe/cab cab troo! Featosi aaaa! Then the lights came.

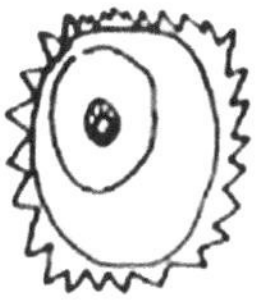

"Boy! How did you just know a long code?" asked alen 6. "Note pad from our tab, now let's go inside!" said alen 10. So anyway they found pearl.

That means.... remember? I said that I will show how the pearls looks like when they find it? Will I keep my promise! So 123 here you go...

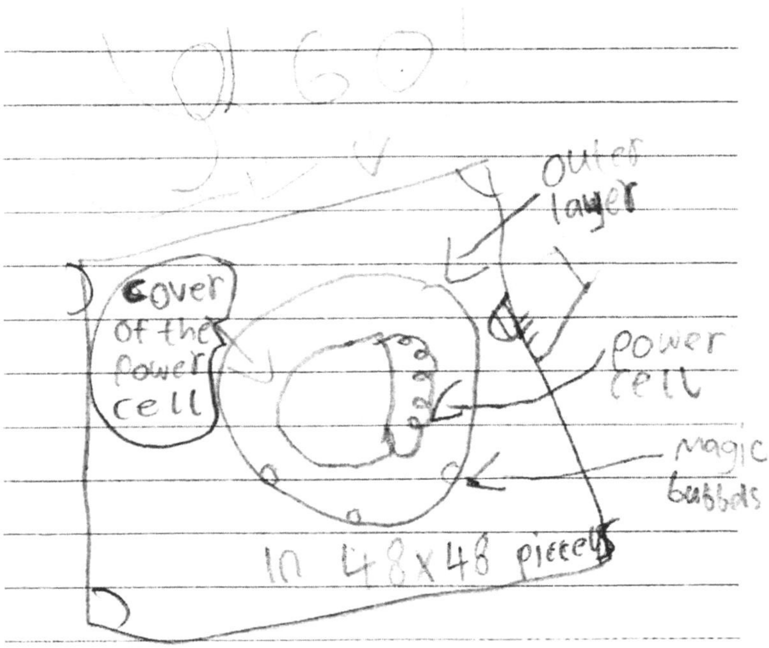

Ok, so now you understand how rare is the pearl.

Now, because of the information, earth is turning into a crazy battle field. People are blaming on others. But it is not their mistake. They do look smarter anymore: the people are not like people, they are like lunatic animals. Do you know who transformed the humans into lunatic animals? Well it was..... 2 persons and a maniac. Don't worry this is a hint to find out the guys who was responsible for this.

(Answer key in next page.)

Ok so if you don't know the answer then here is the answer key 3.2.1....

Go! Please do not copy the answer or you are not a fair reader.

The two persons = Astros and cyborg.

Maniac = the alens most likely alen 1

Surprised on the first question? Well, there is a reason to the answer. Now explain your reason why?

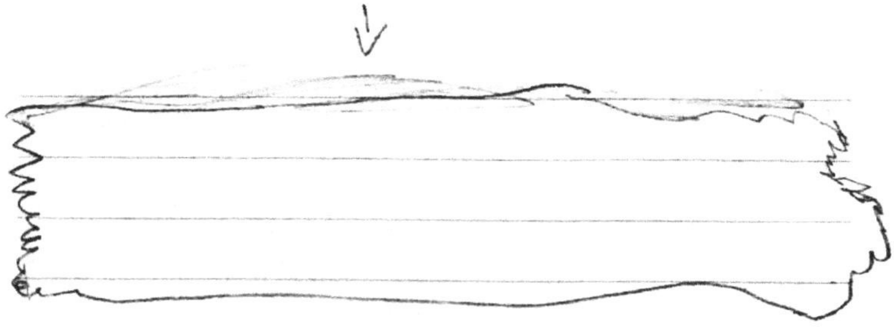

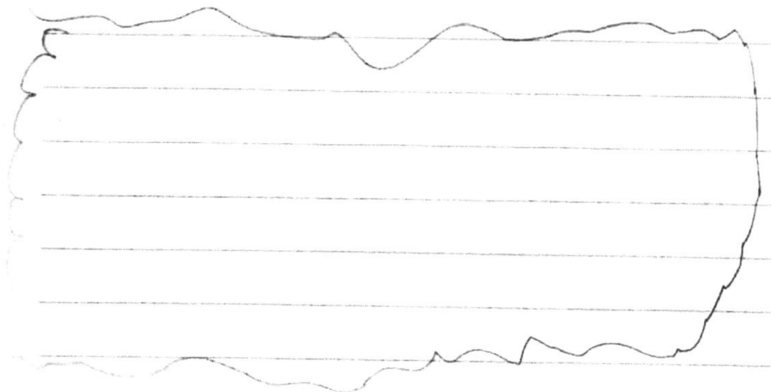

So anyway, back to the alens. They went down to the basement. "Ummm...... leader?", said one of the crew (alens). "What?", said alen 1. "Are there bats or dinosaurs or alen zombies ?", asked alen 6. "Alen 6.... Is this a joke?? Bats don't live on this planet! And secondly, there are no dinosaurs they have been extinct 65 million years ago! They don't live here anyway! And thirdly, what are alen Zombies ? Are you kidding me? there is no such things".

As alen zombies (related to third book "Unsetetobole-the clash of the alen zombies : part one")

Alen 1 will be wrong in 2023, because as this book is published in 2021, in two more years he will be wrong: actually he will get the blame for this! But that won't happen because he is the leader of the alens planet and nobody can do anything about it. He can say whatever he wants as he is the leader and the president of the planet but now he is very angry.

"I should have just hired a new set of crew! I had enough after your unbelievable excuses! This is not a movie! it's a book! I am not moving until I don't hear a single excuse from you ALL!" shouted alen 1 in full anger. Today is not Alen 1's day: he is not in mood. Ok, so meanwhile on earth, the cyborg and the Astros found out that things are getting out of control. The news channels made the cyborg and the Astro realized their mistake and stopped their crazy scary discoveries. They thought that if we stop sending these news on alens then everything will be fine.

Yeah, Earth will not be a lunatic place. What could be possibly wrong if we stop passing the news about alens? Well it will come true soon.... Ha! don't listen to the narrator, reader ! He is probably joking! WHAT??? SERIOUSLY, I AM NOT JOKING..

Chapter 2

THE ONE BLOCK CONVERTER

The alens finally made no noise, no excuses, and no trouble! "Ok fine, we will go", said alen 1. Then a big flash of glistening light flashed through the cave. It was so bright they couldn't see a thing but after a few minutes, the light stopped and revealing the secret to open the darkness in the room. And soon.... "Welcome to my rooms guys! Oh my God! Its look like a rich place! Yep!" said alen 7.

The Place:

Well, you see that rectangular shape between the furnace and soft carpet?

If you think it is a box then you are wrong it may look like a box.........

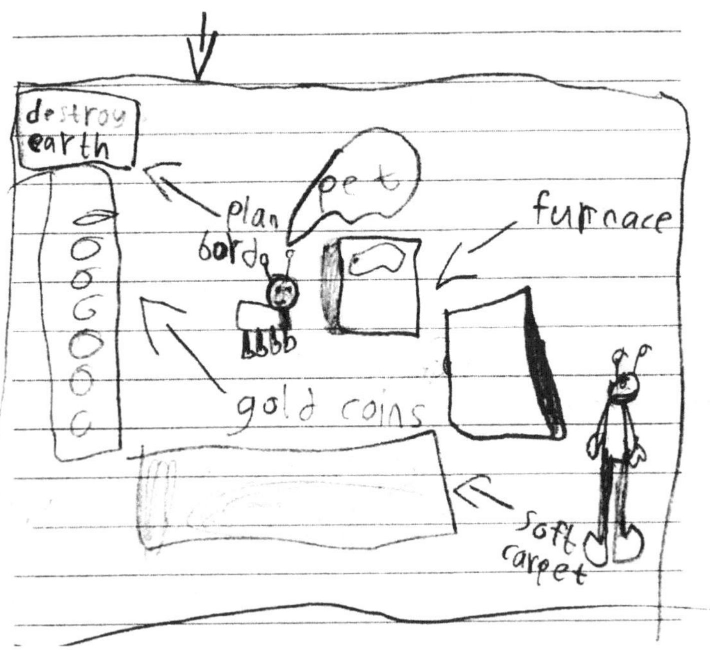

But there is a hidden button next to the thing if you found it then you are very smart tick yes or no if you found it or explain.

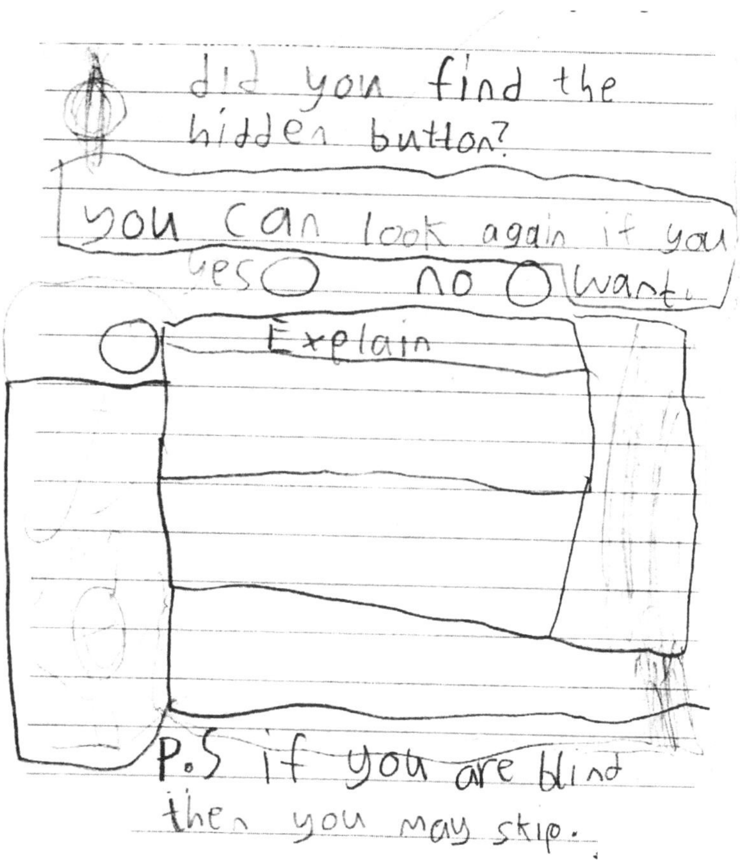

Anyway the alens put their items. I by alen!

Alen 1, will say who will drop items first:

Alen 2, Diamonds! Alen 2 dropped diamonds.

Alen 3, Pearl! Alen 3 dropped the pearl.

Alen 4, Goggles! Alen 4 dropped the goggles.

Alen 5, Iron! Alen 5 dropped the iron.

"Um boss?", asked alen 3. "Are you forgetting something? Because I think you are forgetting something". "Oh don't be a flat bunk!", said alen 1. "We are not forgetting something! Wake up! Seriously

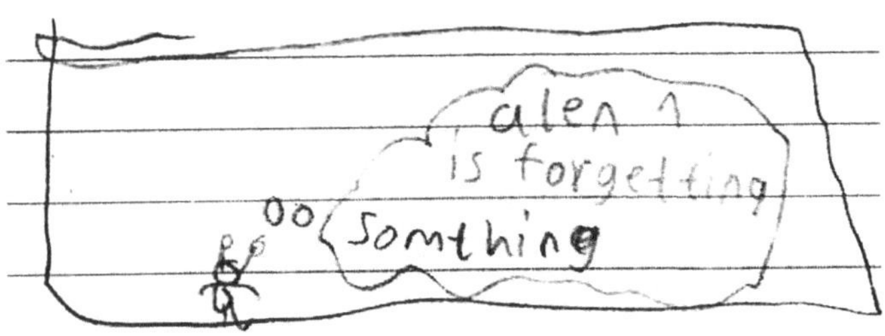

Guys! How about a flash back! Yes I am not joking. A rewind to page 3, it is telling of what they need. Alen 1 is forgetting one thing and that thing is..... colour dye! The weapon will be plain grey. (I promise I will show the weapon in full colour. Not a lie, I can prove it when they found it no joke). So that's why they need the colour dye. But not useful in battling earth and the cyborg but will be difficult because evil will never win! And you know that.

Alen 1 when he was kid

So forgot about that! Now alen 1 picked up the items and ..... Alen 1 forgot something again, but what? "Well, um uh.... Boss!", said alen 6. "You are forgetting something!". "Argh! AGAIN???? What??? Impossible!", shouted alen 1. Actually alen 1 is forgetting something well a page hint! But what page? Well.... I have a hint! Yes a hint. But the hint is related to maths. It's an easy peasy one. It's like kg! No No! Not weight kg. I meant class KG! Yep you know it, I know it. It's none other than kindergarten!

Easy!!!!!!!!

THE NEXT 50

Knew you know it! So anyway the hint is in page 12(-) 6? See told you! You know it! the answer will be shaded! You have to guess the number ok....

Here it goes....

Yep! The answer is....6! Page 6, a paper fell down in the middle of their work! The strange letter was talking about a new ore! Yep.... Now you found what alen 1 has forgotten was 24 pages away! Wow, a long amount for a get away! Anyway.... (Ah! getaway and anyway just rhymed)

Alen 1 realised now what he had forgotten! That's life. Ok fine! Alen 6, ore! Alen 6 dropped the ore.

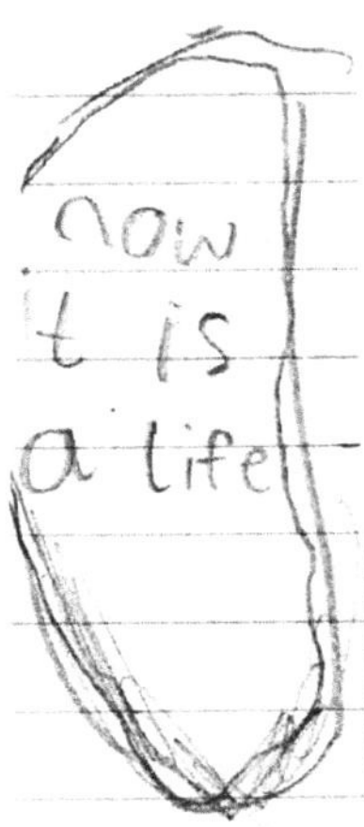

Impossible to remember all the items? But just try to remember a few of them. Fine I will tell you what the items are! First comes the new ore, second is diamond, third is magic pearl, fourth is iron, and finally the magic goggles. See now you know what! But that doesn't mean you are smart and you know the answers. I told them to you!!!! Now alen 1 combined the items with his power but that wasn't to fully do it. Combining wasn't easy you know...... Instead, alen 1 needs help from the crew. Yep, you know it.

Alen 1 is using the enchanter. The enchanter is used for combining the items to make a weapon. If you have enough power.....

"Crew help me for POWER!", said alen 1 to the crew. "Sure!", said the crew. They showed their combined power along with Alen 1 power, but it made an exploding noise..... because too many items were dropped and mixed. But the enchanter can still handle it!

Then a strange countdown came out of nowhere! It could be a bomb that can destroy the basement. It can be 99% a bomb exploding that could form fire balls but not not as loud. Like if someone says drinking lava is possible that person is 100% insane. Yep we know that. Like that, alen crew will think it is an atomic bomb rolling out of nowhere saying "5 seconds to explode atomic bomb but it is a "misprediction". The timer was a bomb!.

The timer stopped! Well that gave hope and the one block converter was made! Well game over on earth! Well it won't stop cyborg! "Excellent! Now time for one planet to pay the prize!", Said alen 1. So alen 1 took his all mighty weapon and "Boss!!", said alen 5, "What do you want this time?", said alen 1. "How to get to earth? We don't have a spaceship!". "Oh brother! We don't need one! Let me show you a magic trick to get there without it!", said alen 1. He will now show the steps of how to go to earth without spaceship.

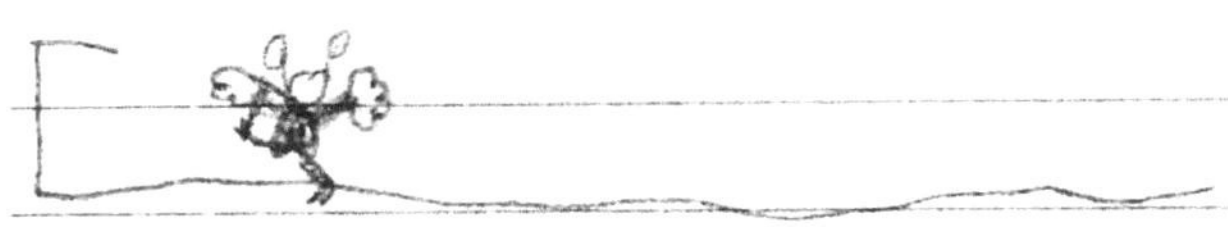

But the first step will look dumb as it is... you will think that it's crazy to have steps between planets. Well let's continue it. "Step 1: Fall into the void 3 times! But the good news is that you can respawn. Just like games", said alen 1. "Step 2: After you did step 1 say this code 1234 aw. It won't take long before you FLY! Yes. Step 3: Wait 1 hour and you can fly", said alen 1. See! The creator need license! like this one:

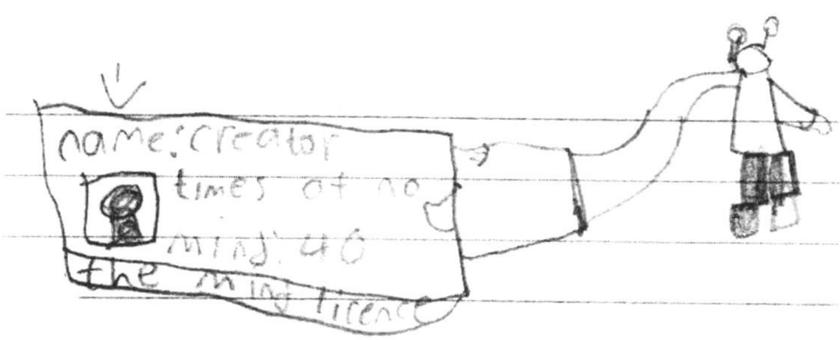

Anyway the alens followed the steps, they fell into the void getting a free fall AHHAHHHOOOO.... The alens screamed, 3 times! and 3 times respawned! Now for step 2 say the code 1234aw. So the alens said the code but then the alens found that they can guide up in the air, but they cannot move in the air. They can only move up and down but not too down or they will go into the danger zone called THE VOID. But now time for step 3: wait 1 hour doing nothing except sleeping or......

The hour will be called the boring hour, you are only enabled to sleep not anything else. "But boss! Will it be even boring to do nothing?", asked alen 3. "Of course not, at least there is a possibility to do our work! which is to rest after all those hard work! You already know how long it took to finally finish this work! One hour is just good enough for our work BREAK. You also know how much items we needed to create the God weapon! I hope you finally understand this heaven! Please you know how angry I was in page 20! I had enough after your excuses".

Now in this one hour you have to keep your make mouth SHUT NOW! Or I'll make you fall out in the universe void! Where you cannot respawn, instead you will be in a jail made out of hard steel and that is none other than the only bed rock! In minecraft, bed rock cannot break! Not even an enchanted diamond pickaxe can break bed rock. It is an illuminati! And OP and God! The void in minecraft is the same as bed rock. ILLUMINATI go to bed rock jail and you will feel the power of

OMAE EN DE SINDRU

Let's go now! One hour has already passed! Woah! Alen 1 filled one whole page of rage (page and rage rhyme) so alen 1 and the alens flew to the earth and landed on the moon! Don't worry it is just a joke. A "not laughable joke". But then the cyborg can sense something similar to the alens! Oh the alens are in big trouble! Busted X2! So alen 1 aimed the one block converter towards earth.

Then it said the count down 5... 4... 3... 2... 1... BIZZrrrkk!!!

Now the earth is a big one block...

Earth is a platformer world! But the alens just got busted by the cyborg! Then the space shuttle took off! And it was a perfect one. Then Astros looked out in the window and found the alens. "Um... cyborg?", asked Astros. "What I see are creepy creatures, and one of them is holding a gun, and it is aiming towards earth". "Who are they? Hmm.... They must be the signal I received here and I don't know who are they. But wait you said that they were holding a gun, and the gun is aiming towards the earth right?", asked the cyborg. "Umm yes", said Astros.

"Wait, so that means.... Oh no..... Something is wrong! Terribly wrong!" "What is it?", asked Astros. "Firstly, we are running out of pages! Secondly those creatures are attacking earth! I know because..... gun=shoot=terrible=end" said cyborg in divided language. "You are right! Now we need to stop them", said Astros. Now... "HEY! YOU GUYS STOP!!! Oh well well, a dummy thing that he is going to defeat me! Ha! I don't think so!" Said alen 1 to the cyborg. "Now I will shoot!" Blizrrrr....! But the cyborg dodged the attack. "GRR! I will defeat you this time!", screamed alen 1 as he aimed at the one block.

Converter, but it was of no use. The cyborg dodged it again "I'll Keeeeel you now", said alen 1, and blasted the one block converter in the power to 11. Lot of power! But the power missed. Alen 1 had seen enough so he went to (not alens planet ok) earth to zap the fire weapon to the people. Then alen 1 stamped on the earth surface (alen 1 is planning to scare the people first then he'll aim). Then after that, alen 1 said in a scary voice: "Oh people...... I am going to get you... So prepare to have a marathon.... Now! Run". The people were so scared, they ran for their life thinking what will happen now ?

Well you don't know how the people listened to alen1 right? Ok I will tell the answer in the end of this novel. People ran very fast as they can. But some of them find a hiding spot. Meanwhile, the cyborg is hiding in a bush trying to find a plan, but then alen 2 attacked the cyborg. "I WILL NOT LET YOU WIN AGAINST OUR BOSS!", shouted alen 2. "Oh yeah?", said the cyborg. Then he fired a laser beam at alen 2. "Ahhhhh!", shouted alen 2, but then alen 2 bumped into alen 1 disturbing him. "Nooooo! What? The weapon is broken! Grrr! I will get you cyborg!", shouted alen 1.

"Yess!, now time to send you guys home. Accept that alen 1, now time to use my teleport power!" Said cyborg. "Now I defeated my first enemy! Now time to prepare for this!", said cyborg as he aimed a gem at the alens (not alen 1 though) then a flash of bright blue light shot came up, then after the light disappeared the alens were gone... but not alen 1. "Now time to deal with you!", said the cyborg as the cyborg kicked the alen 1 with full power. Now alen 1 fell in the void. So this means alen 1 was defeated, and it is the end, but there are more adventures to come in the next novel.

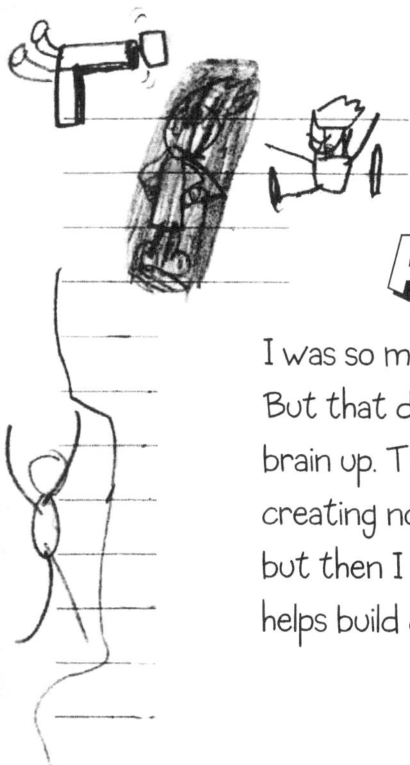

ABOUT THE AUTHOR

I was so much into video games. But that didn't fill my whole brain up. That space was used for creating novels. I never quit gaming but then I found that writing novel helps build creativity than gaming ..

ACKNOWLEDGEMENT

Credit to "Diary of wimpy kid-do it yourself" book for having enough pages for my novel.